CHOUPETTE

'Have no doubt: with company, at events, out walking, at a ball,
even in the academies, cats shall be welcomed, even sought after.
It's impossible to ignore the sense that one's cat is the most agreeable
companion, an admirable pantomime, a born astrologer, a perfect
musician, altogether the very combination of the talents and graces.'

Paradis de Moncrif
Les Chats (Cats), 1727

'Her eyes are like star sapphires.'

CHOUPETTE

THE PRIVATE LIFE OF
A HIGH-FLYING FASHION CAT

Photographs by
Karl Lagerfeld

Compiled by
Patrick Mauriès
and
Jean-Christophe Napias

Thames & Hudson

Design by
Charles Ameline

Additional photographs by
Françoise Caçote
and
Sébastien Jondeau

CONTENTS

VITAL
STATISTICS

Choupette was born

on 15 August 2011. She spent her early months with
Baptiste Giabiconi, a model and singer who received
her as a birthday present in November. At the end of
the same year, before he went away for Christmas,
Baptiste entrusted Choupette to the care of Karl
Lagerfeld. Two weeks of cat-sitting transformed into
an adoption: Karl Lagerfeld had fallen for the kitten's
charms and asked to keep her. From that moment, he
and Choupette have been practically inseparable.

Name

Choupette

Date of birth

15 August 2011

Breed

Birman

Weight

3.5 kg (7 lb 11 oz)

Height

25 cm (9¼ in) to the shoulder

Fur colour

Baked Alaska

Eye colour

Star sapphire blue

Distinctive features

- *Never goes anywhere without one of her two ladies-in-waiting, Françoise et Marjorie*
- *Has a bodyguard, Sébastien Jondeau*
- *Has a private medical consultant, Dr Yola Horn*
- *Never travels without her custom-made Vuitton and Goyard trunks*
- *Hates having her nails trimmed*
- *Eats at the table from three silver Goyard dishes*
- *Plays with her iPad or shopping bags*
- *Has her own Twitter account and a vast following*

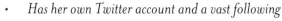

A SACRED CAT

The Birman cat

(also called the Sacred Cat of Burma, but not to be confused with the Burmese) possesses the light golden beige coat, dark points (nose, paws, ears, and tail), and blue eyes characteristic of the Siamese, with the medium-long silky fur of the Persian breed. It is distinguished by its unique, perfectly white feet, and 'gloves' that form a 'V' behind the back paws.

The Birman is medium-to-large in size. Its head is longer than it is wide, with a slightly rounded shape, well-defined full cheeks, and a strong chin. Its large eyes, while not perfectly round, are well-spaced, and invariably blue.

'Affectionate' and 'gentle'
are the two adjectives most commonly used to describe
the Birman. Less docile than a Persian, but calmer
than a Siamese, the Birman is a well-balanced cat. But
that doesn't stop Birmans from being extremely playful. They are sociable and adapt to the life and habits
of their owner. Typically affectionate, sensitive, and
loyal cats, they are not immune, however, to the occasional whim, sulk, or need to be alone for some peace
and quiet.

The exact origins
of the Birman remain a mystery, and speculation about where they hail from has inspired several legends. The best-known story, as told by the novelist Marcelle Adam in the 1920s, whisks the reader off to Burma (now Myanmar). In a temple dedicated to a golden goddess with sapphire eyes, there lived a community of monks and a multitude of cats. The wisest monk, so the story goes, was always accompanied by an all-white cat with topaz eyes named Sinh.

One night, enemies from the kingdom of Siam arrived at the gates of the temple, threatening to profane it and seize its treasures.

In an attempt to ward off the danger, Sinh's old master began to pray so fervently to the goddess that he died on the spot. Leaping to his master's side, Sinh stood over his head and turned to face the goddess with imploring eyes. Then a miracle occurred: his eyes changed to the same colour as those of the goddess and his fur turned golden – all but the paws, which stayed as white as the old monk's hair.

The cat looked toward the temple gates, which the monks – dazzled by what they had just witnessed – managed to shut against the invaders. The temple was saved.

Sinh kept watch over his master's body for seven days and seven nights, with neither food nor water, until he, too, died of sorrow. All of the cats began to reappear in the temple, but the monks saw that they had undergone the same metamorphosis as Sinh: clothed in gold and gloved in white, their eyes had turned to sapphire blue. Thus the Sacred Cats of Burma were born, eventually to be introduced around the world in the 1920s by American and European travellers.

More mundanely, some believe the Birman was born in France in the 1920s as a result of a cross between a Siamese and a Persian; a less poetic story, and one with no more evidence to corroborate its veracity, either.

'Do you know Velázquez's painting Las Meninas, with the Infanta Margarita surrounded by servants? That's Choupette.'

Diego Velázquez, Las Meninas *(The Maids of Honour)*, *1656 (detail)*.

PERSONAL HABITS

'She has lunch and dinner with me,
on the table, with her own dishes.
She never touches my food.
She would never eat on the floor.'

'Cats are committed carnivores.
To stay in shape, they should eat between 30 and 60 per cent
protein every day (meat or fish). The rest should consist
of grains and vegetables. Proteins contain amino
acids, such as taurine or arginine,
which are essential for a cat's well-being.
It's acceptable for cats to eat throughout the day.
In general, unfortunately, they don't drink enough.
However, if a cat does drink a lot, it may be
a symptom that requires attention:
it could indicate a kidney problem.
So it's important to monitor a cat's
eating and drinking habits carefully.'

Doctor
Yola Horn

Regular meals

'She always has five dishes to choose from:
two kinds of dry food,
chicken pâté,
and croquettes
with a turkey or a fish sauce.'

'She doesn't steal food from off your plate.'

Special treats

'Caviar should be limited to tiny quantities, since it's too salty: it
can cause hypertension and eventually induce kidney failure.'

'60 grams (2 oz) of meat or fish
and 60 grams (2 oz) of asparagus tips or baby leeks.'

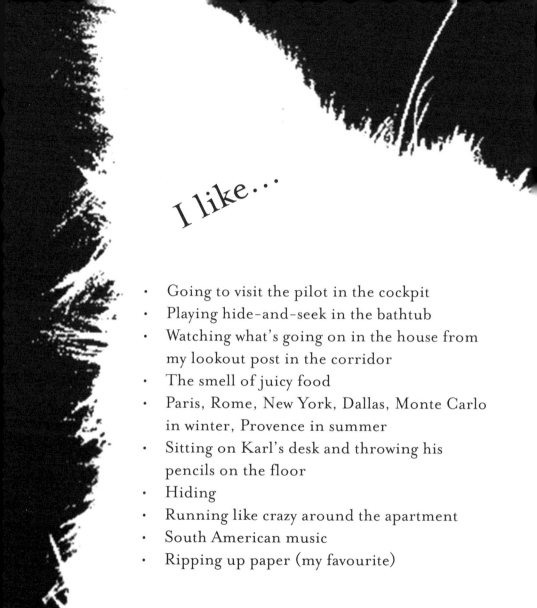

I like...

- Going to visit the pilot in the cockpit
- Playing hide-and-seek in the bathtub
- Watching what's going on in the house from my lookout post in the corridor
- The smell of juicy food
- Paris, Rome, New York, Dallas, Monte Carlo in winter, Provence in summer
- Sitting on Karl's desk and throwing his pencils on the floor
- Hiding
- Running like crazy around the apartment
- South American music
- Ripping up paper (my favourite)

I don't like...

- Taking off and landing (I stay in my bag)
- Room sprays and atomizers
- Shrill voices
- Perfume
- Water (and getting wet)
- Opera

CHOUPETTE'S RECIPES

What domestic feline

can boast, in addition to two ladies-in-waiting and a bodyguard, her own accredited chef? Choupette can, of course. Her chef's name is Patrice; he oversees the meal preparation for the master of the house and gives equal care to its nonchalant Princess. But what about when Choupette dines out? Without strictly limiting herself to five-star establishments, she naturally has her regular haunts (which also happen to be those of her master). The chefs at a number of prestigious establishments – from Café de Flore to Colette, from Le Voltaire to Kinugawa – agree to play along, creating recipes that are guaranteed to bring variety to the everyday fare of a far-from-everyday cat, and which will surely please the average cat.

NIKU SHIGURENI
BY CHEF OZURU,
KINUGAWA

Ingredients

100 g (3 ½ oz) beef fillet
5 cl (scant ¼ cup) light soy sauce
5 cl (scant ¼ cup) mirin
1 small piece of fresh ginger, peeled

Preparation

Finely slice the beef into small pieces. Place the meat in a saucepan with a little cold water and bring to a boil. When the meat begins to change colour, transfer it to a separate saucepan adding the soy sauce and mirin; cook on low heat. Meanwhile, julienne the fresh ginger, slicing it into a dozen very fine slivers, and add it to the saucepan with the meat. Reduce the liquid until it evaporates, then remove the saucepan from the heat to cool. Serve lukewarm.

CHOUPETTE'S EGG FROM LE VOLTAIRE

Ingredients

100 ml (scant ½ cup) milk

1 medium egg

10 fresh mint leaves

4 or 5 green beans, steamed

10 g (2 teaspoons) roasted chicken breast

10 g (2 teaspoons) crabmeat

4.5 g (1 teaspoon) sodium-free mayonnaise

Preparation

In a small saucepan, heat 500 ml (2½ cups) water with the milk. When it comes to a boil, submerge the egg and mint leaves. Cook for nine minutes.

Meanwhile, finely slice four or five green beans and dice the chicken. Combine the sliced green beans, chicken and crabmeat in a salad bowl.

Turn off the heat and remove the egg; run it under cold water, peel it, and then place it back into the mint infusion.

Once the egg has cooled, cut it in half. Remove the yolk and add this to the chicken mixture.

Add the mayonnaise, mash lightly and mix thoroughly.

Chop the egg whites and place them on the serving plate, topping with three quenelles (rounded spoonfuls) of the chicken mixture. Serve immediately.

With thanks to Louis, Titi and Himalaya.

FRESH WATER COCKTAIL FROM THE WATER BAR AT COLETTE

Ingredients

At room temperature:
One bottle of Chantemerle (France)
One bottle of Fashion (Austrian Alps)
One bottle of Malmberg (Sweden)
One carton of Aquapax (Germany)
One bottle of Blue Keld (UK)

Preparation

Fill a glass one quarter full with Chantemerle. Add an equal dash from each of the other four waters and stir gently for a few seconds.

Decant into a bowl and serve immediately.

CHICKEN EN GELÉE
WITH ASPARAGUS

Ingredients

One large carrot
Two asparagus spears (tips only)
One chicken thigh

Preparation

Dice the carrot into small cubes. Chop the asparagus tips into short lengths. Place the chicken thigh, diced carrot, and asparagus into a small saucepan. Add enough water to cover, bring to a boil, then cover and let simmer for 30 minutes, skimming regularly.

Remove from the heat and set aside to cool.

Remove the chicken from the bone and chop finely. In a ramekin, combine the chicken, carrots, asparagus, and remaining cooking juices from the saucepan.

Refrigerate for several hours. Turn the contents of the ramekin out onto a plate; allow time to reach room temperature before serving.

CROQUETTES
À LA CHOUPETTE

Ingredients

1 can sardines in spring water (sodium-free)
five green olives, pitted and finely chopped
pinch of thyme
1 medium-sized carrot, boiled and finely chopped
60 g (½ cup) wheat germ
60 g (½ cup) cornmeal
flour (for sprinkling on pan)

Special Equipment

Small fish-shaped mould or cookie cutter

Preparation

Preheat the oven on medium heat (180°C/350°F).

Using a fork, mash the sardines and mix together with the chopped, pitted olives. Add the thyme and chopped carrot, followed by the wheat germ. Using your fingers, blend well before adding the cornmeal. Continue to blend until the mixture has an even, firm consistency. Use the cutter to form little fish shapes, using all of the mixture.

Place the fish shapes on an oven tray lined with greaseproof paper, lightly dusted with flour, and bake in the preheated oven for about 25 minutes or until the croquettes turn golden brown. Remove from the oven and cool. Serve at room temperature.

KING CRAB
FROM THE
MAISON DU CAVIAR

Ingredients

1 Alaskan King Crab leg
Vegetable stock (sodium-free),
made with celery, bay leaf, thyme,
lavender, carrot rounds
1 very thin slice of Scottish smoked salmon
6–8 caviar eggs

Special Equipment

Lobster crackers and shellfish pick
Crab-shaped mould

44

Preparation

Poach the crab leg in the stock for 10 minutes and set aside to cool.

Cut up the smoked salmon into tiny pieces. Remove the crab meat from the shell with the crackers and pick; chop finely. Mix the crab with the smoked salmon in a bowl. Place the mixture into the crab-shaped mould, filling generously. Add two 'eyes' made of the caviar eggs.

Note: cats can tolerate only minute amounts of fat and salt, so the quantities of salmon and caviar must be tiny.

DECONSTRUCTED 'CHOUPETTE' CLUB SANDWICH FROM THE CAFÉ DE FLORE

Ingredients

½ slice of white bread, crust removed
Small piece of roasted chicken breast
1 lettuce leaf
1 cherry tomato
½ hard-boiled egg
1 small piece of lean bacon (well done)
1 teaspoon mayonnaise

Preparation

Dice the bread and the cooked chicken. Chop the lettuce leaf coarsely. Slice the cherry tomato into quarters. Chop the hard-boiled egg and bacon finely. Mix these ingredients together before stirring in the mayonnaise. Serve immediately at room temperature.

Note: if desired, the mixture may be set in a small ramekin and turned out onto a serving plate.

JET-SETTER

As everyone knows,
cats are not natural travellers. They are homebodies;
they like their own space and routine. Leaving home
can therefore often be difficult, and cats tend to hunker
down in their travel case. But what would Choupette
be without Karl, or he without her? In the end, the
Princess had to come to terms with accompanying
her master, the Flying Couturier, on his constant trips
that take him from Rome to Monte Carlo, and from
New York to Milan via Dallas. But being an out-of-
the-ordinary sort of cat, Choupette only leaves home
with her custom-made luggage and accompanied either
by her lady's maid Françoise Caçote or her bodyguard Sébastien Jondeau, and preferably by private
jet. Among other special privileges, she is allowed to
stroll freely around the cabin, and likes nothing better
than to visit the pilot in the cockpit, or simply to sit
quietly and contemplate the blue of the sky through
the window.

'When we go on a trip, Choupette has almost as
many bags as Mr Lagerfeld. I'm not exaggerating:
her litter tray, a fresh litter bag for each day, all of her food,
bags of toys and beauty products — eye drops, and brushes for her
wonderful fur — and a travel case specially made
for her by Goyard, for enjoying her meals
while she is on the plane.'

BEAUTY
REGIME

'It has been observed that —
of all the creatures — women, flies,
and cats spend the most time
attending to their appearance.'

Charles
Nodier
(1780–1844)

'A cat should be brushed
every other day, to avoid knots,
but also to avoid fur balls
and other digestive problems
caused by hair swallowed
when they lick themselves.'

Doctor
Yola Horn

'Choupette, I declare you charm me true:
No Tom could show a bolder heart
Nor Cat a finer form, than you.
But tell me:
Aren't you just a little inclined to flirt?'

Freely adapted from the Epistle of Tata,
the Marquise de Monglas's Tomcat,
to Grisette, Madame Deshoulières's Cat, *1678*

57

FASHION MUSE

In sync with the spirit
of her times, Choupette has appeared all over the web,
on innumerable computer screens, smartphones, and
on countless social network postings. But — living as
she does with someone who harbours a vast appetite
for images — it was inevitable that she would come
into the focus of the fashion photographer's lens. She
began by posing with and for Karl, before becoming
a model in her own right. It was equally destined that
Choupette would work only with fashion's most revered
supermodels.

Choupette's first shoot took place in Paris, one
warm summer evening, on a terrace overlooking the
Seine and the Eiffel Tower. For the September 2012
issue of *V* magazine, Karl Lagerfeld chose to recreate a
sensual setting worthy of the Romantic poet Baudelaire
in a suite at the Shangri-La Hotel for a truly radiant
pair: the luscious Laetitia Casta and Choupette.

An appearance with Linda Evangelista – 'a Stra-divarius violin', as Karl unforgettably described her – followed in the July 2013 edition of German *Vogue*. In black and white, against a plain, unadorned wall, with deep shadows and rich contrasts between dark-haired Linda dressed in black, and Choupette's immaculate fur, this was nothing less than a return to the highest order of Hollywood glamour.

What followed was unstoppable: article after article, appearances in the most prestigious fashion pages: *i-D*, *Vogue*, *L'Officiel*, *Harper's Bazaar* … and like any superstar model, Princess Choupette was soon commanding covers, in print and online. By this point, a book deal was the logical next step.

For *Numéro Homme*'s October 2013 issue, Karl and Choupette posed for Pierre et Gilles in their Pré-Saint-Gervais studio. The photo ('For Your Eyes Only') was featured in the 'Heroes' exhibition at the Daniel Templon gallery in Paris in April 2014.

For the photo, they explained, Karl Lagerfeld assumes the look of 'a James Bond character, in a scene inspired by the film *Men in Black*.'

Karl Lagerfeld is a regular visitor to the Shu Uemura cosmetics boutique on boulevard Saint-Germain in Paris. This may sound surprising to those who don't know that he uses their eye shadows and pencils instead of watercolours or pastels to colour his drawings. 'No other manufacturer makes such beautiful colours,' he says.

In 2012, he linked up with the Japanese brand to create a cosmetics range called 'Mon Shu Girl'. A new range with a new muse was launched in 2014, with Choupette inspiring her new line, 'Shu-Pette', which features a custom eye shadow created in homage to Choupette's eyes. Blue, naturally.

ESSENTIAL ACCESSORIES

'Choupette is really famous.
She has become the most
famous cat in the world.'

Tokidoki is an LA-based, Japanese-inspired brand dreamed up by Italian artist Simone Legno in 2005. She has millions of fans all over the world. In 2013, Tokidoki and Karl got together to create a capsule collection of clothes and playful accessories. Choupette was naturally involved in the whole adventure, and was immortalized as a collector's figurine. Apparently, she rather likes it (see p. 70).

For the launch of the Karl × Tokidoki collection, Choupette and her master became the heroes of a two-minute animated feature showing them around the world: Paris, Rome, London, Berlin, St Petersburg, China, Australia, the United States.... They travel hanging from the stem of a giant daisy, in a horse-drawn carriage, on the back of a dragon, on a flying carpet, and even inside a bubble!

Shin Tanaka, the Japanese 'paper toy' star, combines the art of origami with urban culture. At the end of 2013, in a touring exhibition called 'Paper Toy Mania', he portrayed a range of characters inspired by Karl Lagerfeld's world, including Choupette — always shown close to her master, and even sporting his legendary dark glasses.

Choupette clearly deserved her own collection. And sure enough, at the end of 2013, a capsule collection was launched in Karl Lagerfeld boutiques in Paris, Berlin, Munich, Amsterdam, Antwerp, Beijing, and Shanghai. The accessories range — almost exclusively black and white — features Choupette's pointed ears and whiskers, and includes a cap, a scarf, a tote bag, a key ring, and even an iPad case.

'She likes strange toys,
toys that aren't supposed to be toys.
She plays with pieces of wood,
scraps of paper,
and shopping bags.
She loves shopping bags,
especially when they have ribbons.'

CHOUPETTE
BLUE

Like every Birman,

Choupette's eyes are blue. The particular hue gave Karl Lagerfeld the chance to understand the true meaning of 'star sapphire blue', or, as he says, 'chalcedony blue'. These subtle shades allude to the jewelry of Suzanne Belperron, whose work he has collected for many years. Since nothing is ever irrelevant in the life of a designer, this colour has become a source of inspiration. Guests attending the Chanel Haute Couture spring/summer 2012 collection couldn't miss the prevalence of a certain shade of blue that was also featured in the ready to wear spring/summer 2013 collection. And the lucky few who were invited to the Métiers d'Art 2014 presentation in Dallas nearly drowned in an ocean of blue, ranging from the lightest to darkest hues ... 'Blue,' explained the smitten designer, 'is the colour of the air, the sky ... and the eyes of a certain little cat.'

'... the eyes of a certain little cat': this statement by
Karl Lagerfeld didn't go unnoticed in the wings of the
Chanel catwalk show.

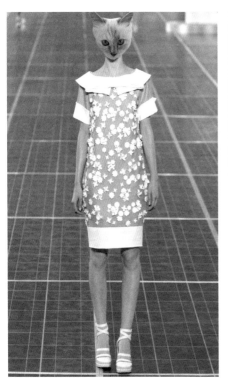 

And those who saw the collection in Paris were seeing blue — in a palette of more than one hundred shades.

But did they suspect that Choupette's eyes were the inspiration?

85

'Choupette isn't a typical
Chanel woman.
She's more
Jean Harlow.'

CHOUPETTE ON THE NET

Choupette is the first representative of a new species: the e-cat. Since 2012 photos showing her playing on an iPad have been all over the web, lending her own particular class to the cat superstars of the digital era. Now Choupette appears on tens of thousands of Internet pages. Curious viewers can even see her in action, in clips posted on YouTube.

A Twitter account was next, and quickly attracted tens of thousands of followers. She features in innumerable Facebook pages, Tumblr accounts, and a series of Choupette emoticons ... It's a sure bet that she'll continue to embrace every form of technological innovation. Is Choupette a Cybercat?

Choupette made her world debut at 11:15 am on 15 January 2012 when famous fashion editor Stephen Gan tweeted:

'Karl Lagerfeld's Sunday night photo: meet Choupette, his new kitten. — SG'

The tweet was illustrated by a photo taken at Karl Lagerfeld's home. Choupette was five months old.

Only a few months later, it was Choupette's turn to tweet:

6 June 2012, 7:12 am —
'Baptiste may think he is a muse but only I, Choupette, am Lagerfeld's true muse. Everything from my whiskers 2 my meows inspire.'

It's been whispered that, because she is so busy, Choupette couldn't possibly be the author of this account, and that actually she's hiding behind Ashley Tschudin. That hasn't stopped her from attracting a huge crowd of eager followers, who include Inès de la Fressange and a certain Karl Lagerfeld.

Choupette Lagerfeld @ChoupettesDiary · 6 juin 2012
Baptiste may think he is a muse but only I, Choupette, am Lagerfeld's true muse. Everything from my whiskers 2 my meows inspire,

Réduire   ← Répondre   t♻ Retweeter   ★ Favori   ••• Plus

RETWEETS   FAVORIS
17   7

07:12 - 6 juin 2012 · Détails

Choupette doesn't have an Instagram account, but Karl does, and he regularly posts photos of his beloved Princess. Since everyone seems to fall for her charm, Choupette's regular attendants Françoise and Sébastien post their own photos too, with an occasional flurry of selfies, from on board the plane or elsewhere, keeping eager fans up-to-date with the latest on the most famous cat in the world.

In early 2014, at the launch of two new fragrances – one for men, one for women – Karl Lagerfeld introduced EmotiKarl, a free app for iPhone and iPad users. It features dozens of Tokidoki-inspired emoticons, including six different Choupette faces, like an oriental goddess in multiple incarnations.

THE ARTIST AND THE PUSSYCAT

Quiet and solitary,
curious and discreet, the cat seems naturally suited as
the emblem of the writer, or the artist in general; a
delicate hybrid combining the cerebral and the sensual,
as in the first stanza of 'The Cats' by Charles Baudelaire:

> *Both passionate lovers and austere scholars*
> *Love, when they reach advanced years,*
> *Cats, strong and gentle, pride of the house,*
> *Who, like them, feel the cold, and prefer to stay put.*

As well as the famously cat-loving author of *Les Fleurs
du Mal*, a host of artistic and literary felinophiles come to
mind – including Manet, and the writers Champfleury
and Pierre Loti. In the twentieth century, Colette and
Jean Cocteau shared walks with their wise companions

in the gardens of the Palais Royal; and Parisians would often see Paul Léautaud (a Voltaire scholar and author of a journal much favoured by Karl Lagerfeld) leaving his office at the *Mercure de France* near the Place Saint-Sulpice, weighed down with a bag of offal from the butcher's.

The Anglo-Saxons have been no less felinophile, from the smiling Cheshire Cat to Doris Lessing's semi-feral cats (she wrote a classic cat memoir in 1967). Edward Lear, the foremost poet of nonsense verse of his time and the inventor of the limerick, gave us 'The Owl and the Pussy-cat', cherished by every self-respecting cat-lover. The last of twenty-one children, with a tendency to asthma and to epilepsy, Lear lived with a sister 21 years his senior until her death when he was in his fifties. Lear began his career as an ornitholo-gical painter. His first book was on parrots, following which he launched himself on long expeditions to the Far East and the Levant, where he made many paintings and engravings.

Lear published his first *Book of Nonsense* in 1846 before creating a long line of imagined creatures such as the Pobble and the Jumblies (which Edward Gorey would illustrate a century later). Nursing an unrequited passion for his friend Franklin Lushington, and afflicted with various ailments, Lear did not lead a happy life, but drew strength equally from his skills as an artist and a writer. He retired to San Remo in the 1870s, living out his last years in the company of his cat Foss, a philosopher cat, who was given a full funeral in the gardens of Lear's Italian villa in 1886.

Speculation on the characteristics that link most of the figures mentioned hereafter may be best left to psychologists. From graphic artists Saul Steinberg and Edward Gorey to Dorothy Parker – who shared not only a passion for cats but also a certain taste for irony and amused detachment – they manifest the absurd in all its forms, and with a healthy dose of humour, preferably black.

Fob dansant

FROM 'THE OWL AND THE PUSSY-CAT'

The Owl and the Pussy-cat went to sea
*   In a beautiful pea green boat,*
They took some honey, and plenty of money,
*   Wrapped up in a five-pound note.*
The Owl looked up to the stars above,
*   And sang to a small guitar,*
'O lovely Pussy! O Pussy, my love,
*   What a beautiful Pussy you are,*
*   You are,*
*   You are!*
What a beautiful Pussy you are!'

Edward Lear, 1871

*Foss
rampant*

Foss, a untin.

Foss Couchant

'I never had the imagination to give
my cats names: they were always
just Moumoutte, and their kittens
were invariably Mimi.
And really in the end, for me there
are no other names more suitable,
or more cat-like, than those
two adorable ones:
Mimi and Moumoutte.'

PIERRE LOTI

Pierre Loti with his cats in his garden in Rochefort, 1907.

Facing page (left): Colette.
(right): Colette's hand.
Photographs by Walter Rimot.

Below: Paul Léautaud and his cats.
Photograph by Robert Doisneau.

*'There is no such thing
as an ordinary cat.'*

COLETTE

'*I love cats because I love my house,*
and because more and more they
become the soul made visible.'

JEAN COCTEAU

Holly Golightly, the chic and nimble-footed heroine of *Breakfast at Tiffany's*, met a little cat by the river whom she chose to call – prosaically, perhaps, or as a minimalist before her time – 'Cat'.

He comes across as a reflection of Holly, with a lack of attachments characteristic of cats, and which in his case is both half wished for and half tolerated.

*Right: Truman Capote.
Photograph by Steve Schapiro.*

*Facing page: Saul Steinberg
showing his cat how to stretch.
Photograph by
Henri Cartier-Bresson.*

As much as (or perhaps more than) the novella by Truman Capote, Blake Edwards's luminous film version of the book, with its heroine and her little black dress, lingers in the memory. 'Cat' in the film was actually played by Orangey, who was chosen from twenty-five candidates. He became one with the image of Audrey Hepburn (chosen over Marilyn Monroe for the part), who remains the definitive incarnation of Holly Golightly, the essence of feline grace.

Saul Steinberg (1914–1999) was a virtuoso artist who mastered drawing, engraving, collage, and sculpture, succeeding in being both extremely popular and artistically acclaimed. Born in Romania, exiled to Italy, he fled to New York in 1941 to escape fascism. He began his career as an illustrator at the *New Yorker* where he became a central figure, designing over one hundred covers and contributing more than one thousand drawings.

Right: Eames chair decorated by Saul Steinberg. Photograph by Peter Stackpole.

Facing page: Saul Steinberg's cat.

Steinberg's recurrent themes (as noted in a famous text by Roland Barthes) were beaches, the subway, stationery, bars, birds, crocodiles, airmail, abstract painting, Indians, records, parties, bridges, pin-ups, labels, and ... cats.

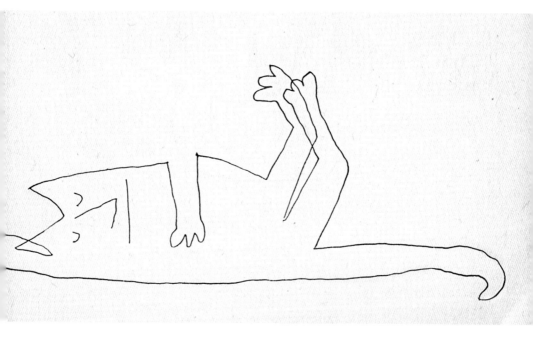

'Steinberg tells how in his house he drew his cat on a wall,' Barthes writes. 'After that the real cat always stayed close to its image.' He concludes: 'Reversal: in Steinberg's world the image tames the thing. (Steinberg's images are familiar animals.)' From *All Except You*, 1983

Like Karl, Dorothy Parker lived in her books.
Like Karl, Dorothy Parker adored her cat.
Like Dorothy Parker, Karl could say:

*'The first thing I do in the morning
is brush my teeth
and sharpen my tongue.'*

Edward Gorey at his house on Cape Cod, 1994.
Photograph by Thibault Jeanson.

There are few cat-lovers who do not display some indifference to convention, not to say a certain eccentricity.

Edward Gorey (1925–2000) was no exception. If there were ever a King of Cats (and a flamboyantly eccentric one at that), it would be this complete artist – draughtsman, writer, ballet-obsessive, stage designer, screenwriter, and puppeteer – whose work is populated by hundreds of cats, and whose most famous book, endlessly reprinted, is titled, appropriately, *Category*.

By far outstripping the impassioned madness of Léonor Fini or Paul Léautaud, Gorey lived in his unconventional Cape Cod den surrounded by a pride of cats that ruled over the house. The cats were the masters, and did as they pleased – including working visitors' scalps with their claws. Obviously, the only possible response was to respect the rules of the household with stoicism.

In 1840, the French publisher Pierre-Jules Hetzel came up with the idea — in reaction to Balzac's *La Comédie Humaine* (The Human Comedy) — of an *Animal Comedy*, illustrated by Grandville and with contributions from some of the greatest authors of the time, starting with Balzac himself. *Peines de coeur d'une chatte anglaise* (Heartaches of an English Pussycat) is probably the best-known of the series of tales that make up the *Scènes de la vie privée et publique des animaux* (Scenes from the Private

Claudie Gastine, Christmas window at Les Galeries Lafayette, Paris, on the theme of Heartaches of an English Pussycat, *1977.*

p. 116 and facing page:
sketches by Grandville for
Heartaches of an
English Pussycat
by Honoré de Balzac.

and Public Lives of the Animals), which appeared in two volumes in 1841 and 1842 after serial publication.

Balzac's story concerns a magnificent English feline heroine, Beauty, whose fur — which is as immaculate as Choupette's — saves her from drowning. Exposed to the attentions of a large Persian tomcat named Puff, she soon falls for the rough charms of Brisquet, a young tom who initiates her in the pleasures of the gutter, with disastrous consequences.

Grandville's drawings prefigure those of the twentieth century, from Benjamin Rabier to Walt Disney. *Heartaches of an English Pussycat* was an instant success. The tales were superbly adapted for the stage by the TSE group in 1980 as *Heartaches of a Pussycat*, whose costumes by Claudie Gastine and Rostislav Dobujinski were unforgettable. Hans Werner Henze turned it into an opera in 1983, *The English Cat*, with an original English libretto by Edward Bond.

Mon silence l'enhardit, et il s'écria : Chère Minette !

'*Choupette
is a woman
spoiled to death.*'

ACKNOWLEDGMENTS

The publishers extend their warmest thanks to Karl Lagerfeld for his help and support for this project from its earliest conception.

Grateful thanks are due to the following, each of whom helped to make publication possible: Françoise Caçote and Sébastien Jondeau, Dr Yola Horn, Marie-Louise de Clermont-Tonnerre and Agnès Duval at Chanel, Jonathan Zlatics at Karl Lagerfeld, Mirjam Schuele, Thibault Jeanson, Sandrine Gulbenkian-Napias, Roxanne Rouffiac and Chef Ozuru at Kinugawa, Antoine Picot at Le Voltaire, Sarah, Guillaume, Sébastien and Marc at chez colette, La Maison du Caviar, and Francis Boussard at Café de Flore.

CREDITS

Sketch after a drawing by Marie Laurencin.

*'One day, I'll do a book,
The Journal of
Choupette.
I'm not Colette,
but we can write a book
about a cat, can't we?'*

On the cover: (front) © Pierre et Gilles
(back) © Karl Lagerfeld

First published in the United Kingdom in 2014 by
Thames & Hudson Ltd, 181A High Holborn,
London WC1V 7QX

Choupette: The Private Life of a High-Flying Fashion Cat © 2014 Thames & Hudson Ltd, London
Text © 2014 Jean-Christophe Napias and Patrick Mauriès
Images © 2014 Karl Lagerfeld, with the exception of those noted on p. 125

British Library Cataloguing-in-Publication Data
A catalogue record for this book is available from
the British Library

ISBN 978-0-500-51774-1

Printed and bound in China by C&C Offset Printing Co. Ltd

To find out about all our publications, please visit **www.thamesandhudson.com**.
There you can subscribe to our e-newsletter, browse or download our current
catalogue, and buy any titles that are in print.